Contents

The lighthouse mystery

An unsolved mystery is a puzzle that has not been solved. There was a mystery at a lighthouse called Eilean Mor. The mystery is still unsolved.

The mystery at the Eilean Mor lighthouse was never solved.

A lighthouse shows boats where there are rocks in the sea. Long ago, people had to live in the lighthouse. They had to look after the lighthouse and keep the light shining. Three men looked after the lighthouse at Eilean Mor.

Three men lived in the Eilean Mor lighthouse.

One Christmas, a boat came to bring food for the men at the lighthouse. When the boat got to the Eilean Mor lighthouse, no one was there.

A boat came to bring Christmas food for the men at the lighthouse.

Where had the three men from the lighthouse gone? The door to the lighthouse was locked. Inside it was clean and bright. The men had left their boat behind. The three men from the lighthouse had vanished. They were never seen again. What happened at Eilean Mor is still a mystery today.

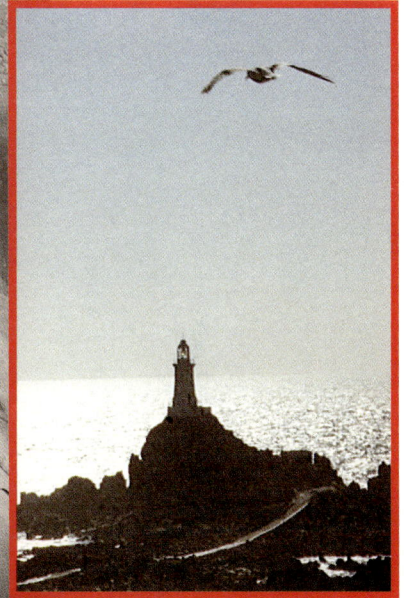

The three men from the lighthouse had vanished!

The lost city

Long ago, there was a great city called Atlantis. We know about Atlantis because people wrote about it many, many years ago. A man called Plato wrote the story of Atlantis.

Plato is the man on the right.

In the story that Plato wrote, the city of Atlantis was splendid. The people who lived there built great houses and temples. Suddenly Atlantis disappeared.

*Atlantis was a splendid city with
great houses and temples.*

Some people think that there was a big volcano near Atlantis. They think that the volcano may have erupted. The ash and lava from the volcano may have covered Atlantis.

Some people think that ash and lava from a volcano may have covered Atlantis.

Many people think that Atlantis is now under the sea. Perhaps a huge wave covered the city. People still look for clues about Atlantis. They want to find the lost city and solve this mystery. How could a big city have disappeared?

Some people think that Atlantis is under the sea.

The Mary Celeste

The Mary Celeste was the name of an old cargo ship. A cargo ship takes heavy loads of cargo from one land to another. More than 100 years ago, the Mary Celeste was sailing across the sea. Something very strange happened to the Mary Celeste on her way across the sea.

Something strange happened to the Mary Celeste.

The Mary Celeste was seen by another ship. She seemed to be sailing around and around in the same place. The other ship sent a message using flags to the Mary Celeste. Nobody answered the message.

The other ship sent a message to the Mary Celeste but nobody answered.

There was no one on the Mary Celeste! All the people on board had vanished. The table was still ready for breakfast.

There were no people on board the Mary Celeste but the table was still ready for breakfast!

No one knows what happened to the people on board the Mary Celeste. They had left so quickly. There were no clues left behind. What do you think might have happened?

What do you think might have happened to the Mary Celeste?

The curse of the Pharaohs

Pharaohs lived in Ancient Egypt. A Pharaoh was a king or queen. There are some strange stories about Pharaohs.

A Pharaoh was a king or queen in Ancient Egypt.

When Pharaohs died, they were put in tombs. Some tombs were in pyramids. Some were under the ground. They were full of treasure. The tombs in the pyramids or under the ground were often robbed for the treasure.

The tombs of the Pharaohs were often robbed for the treasure.

Some people think that the Pharaohs put a curse on their tombs. Two men from Britain went to Egypt to look for ancient tombs. They found the tomb of a boy Pharaoh called Tutankhamen.

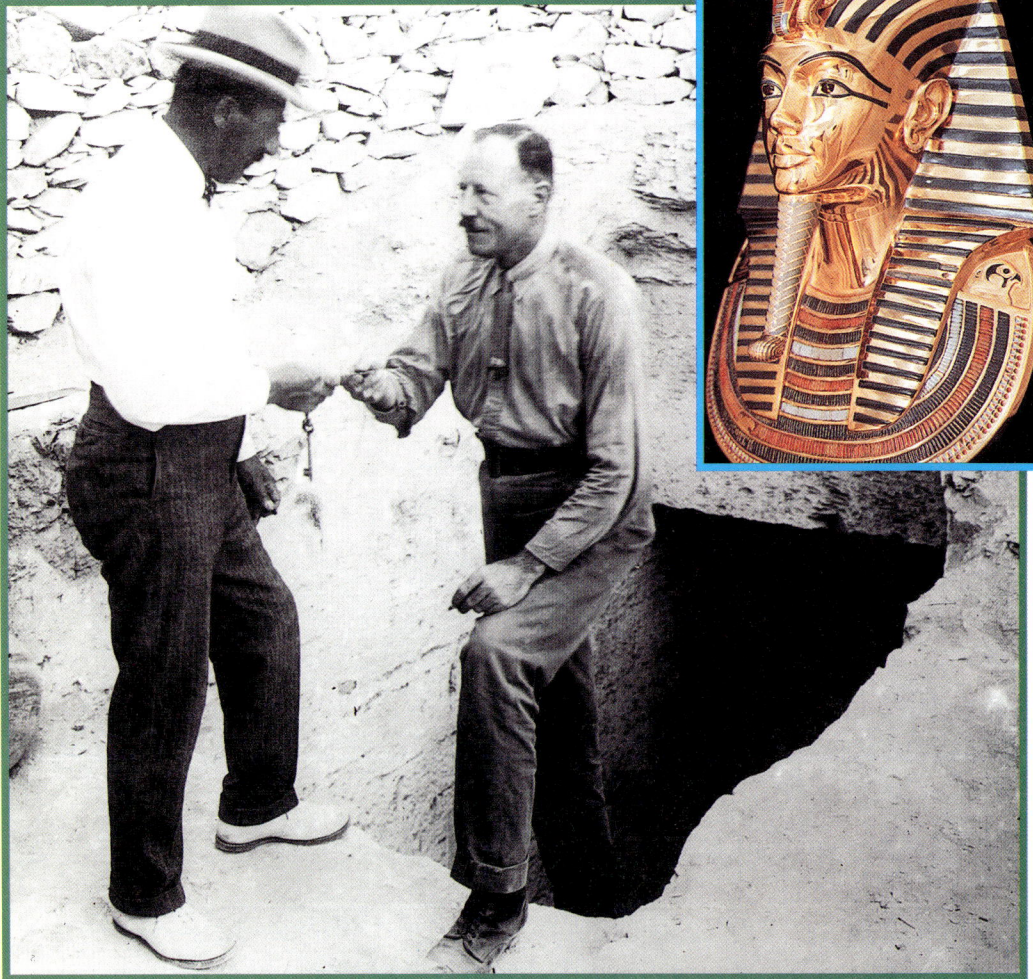

Two men found the tomb of a boy Pharaoh called Tutankhamen.

The two men found lots of great treasure in the tomb of Tutankhamen. Some people were afraid of the tomb. They were scared that the Pharaoh had put a curse on it.

People were scared that the Pharaoh had put a curse on the tomb.

Some strange things happened to the two men. A snake ate the pet bird of one of the men. A little while later, a mosquito bit the other man. He died from this mosquito bite. At the moment the man died, his dog in Britain also died.

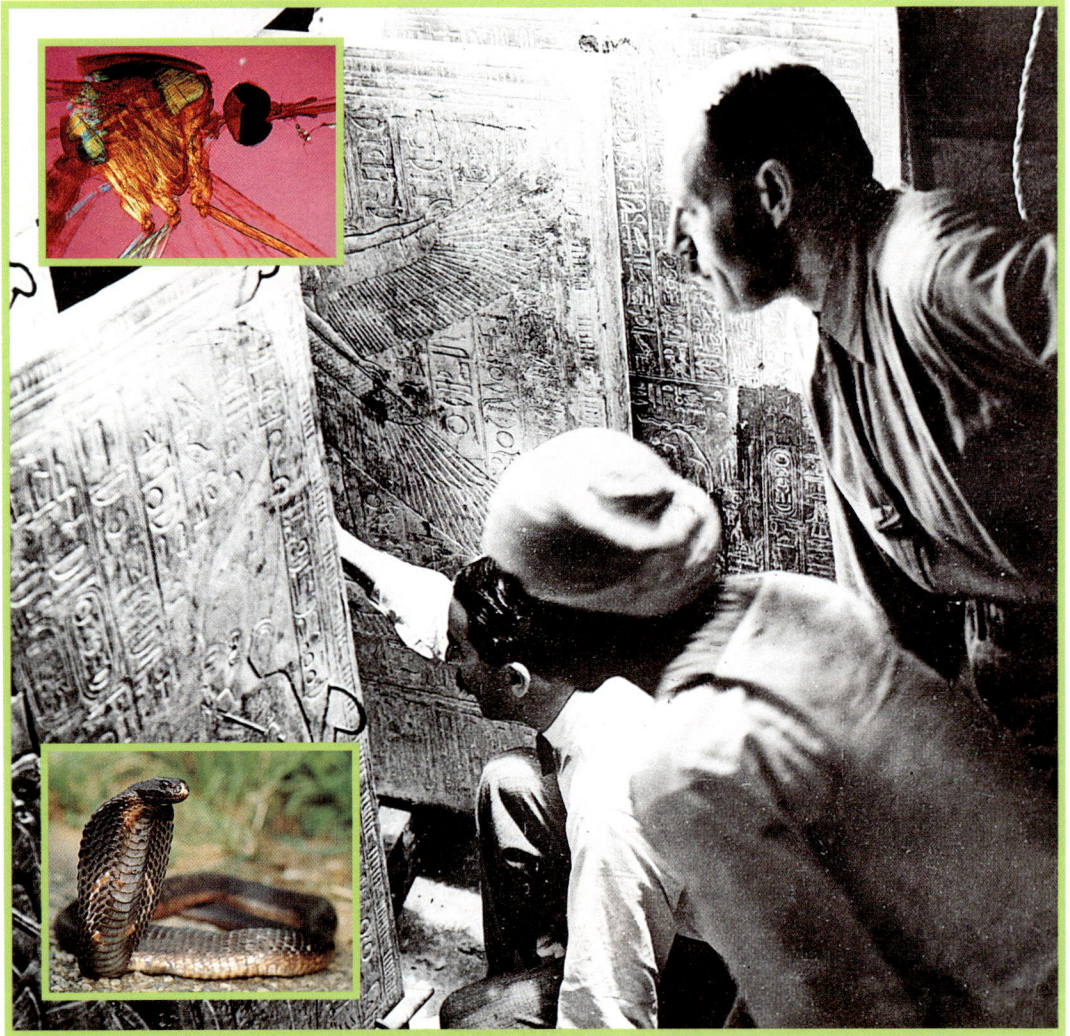

Strange things happened to the men who found the tomb.

At the same moment, all the lights in Cairo went out. Cairo was the city near the tomb of Tutankhamen. Was this the curse of the Pharaohs? Or was the curse just a story to stop the tombs being robbed?

All the lights in Cairo went out.

The Bermuda Triangle

There have been many mysteries near an island called Bermuda. All of these mysteries have happened at sea. This part of the sea is sometimes called the Bermuda Triangle.

*This part of the sea near Bermuda is
sometimes called the Bermuda Triangle.*

Over 500 years ago, a famous sea captain called Christopher Columbus was sailing his boat through the Bermuda Triangle. He saw a great red and yellow ball of fire in the sky. Strange green and yellow clouds have also been seen in the Bermuda Triangle.

Christopher Columbus saw a ball of fire in the sky.

Compasses will not always work in the Bermuda Triangle. Ships and planes need compasses to tell them where they are going.

Compasses will sometimes not work in the Bermuda Triangle.

In the Bermuda Triangle, ships, planes and people have all vanished. Once, five American planes all vanished in the Bermuda Triangle. There are lots of mysteries about the Bermuda Triangle.

Many planes have vanished in the Bermuda Triangle.

Index